Stay Alert, Stay Safe

How to Spot and Stop Scammers

Kenneth Davis

All Right Reserved. No part of this book may be reproduced, stored in a retrieval system, or transmitted in any form or by any means, electronic, mechanical, photocopying, recording, scanning, or otherwise, without the prior written permission of the author and publisher, except for brief quotations embodied in critical reviews and certain other noncommercial uses permitted by copyright law

Copyright © {Kenneth Davis} {2024}

TABLE OF CONTENT

Chapter 1 6

Recognizing the Signs of Online Deception 6

Understanding the Tactics of Social Media Scammers 7

Identifying Fake Profiles: Red Flags to Watch Out For 8

The Art of Emotional Manipulation: How Scammers Target Your Trust 9

Chapter 2 11

Anatomy of a Scam: From Contact to Con 11

Initiating Contact: How Scammers Reach Out to Their Targets 12

Building Trust: The Rapid Rise of Affection and Flattery 12

Moving to Private Platforms: Why Scammers Prefer WhatsApp and Google Chat 13

Chapter 3 15

Tales of Deception: Stories from the Frontlines 15

Military Impostors: The Uniformed Scam Artists 16

Offshore Engineers and Boarding School Children: The Fictional Lives of Scammers 17

The Emotional Rollercoaster: Victims' Experiences of Manipulation and Coercion 18

Chapter 4 20

Protecting Yourself: Strategies for Defense 20

Staying Vigilant: Tips for Recognizing and Avoiding Scams 21

Setting Boundaries: How to Safeguard Your Personal Information 22

Reporting Scammers: Taking Action to Protect Yourself and Others 23

Chapter 5 25

Empowering Resilience: Reclaiming Control 25

Asserting Your Rights: Saying No to Scammers' Demands 26

Rebuilding Trust: Recovering from the Emotional Impact of Deception 26

Moving Forward: Strengthening Your Online Safety Practices 27

Discussion Questions 29

Reflection Essay 32

Chapter 1

Recognizing the Signs of Online Deception

In today's interconnected digital world, the rise of social media platforms has provided ample opportunities for individuals to connect and engage with others from around the globe. However, amidst this virtual landscape lies a lurking danger: online deception. Chapter 1 delves deep into the intricacies of recognizing the signs of online deception, equipping readers with the knowledge and tools necessary to navigate the digital realm safely and securely.

Understanding the Tactics of Social Media Scammers

The chapter commences with an exploration of the various tactics employed by social media scammers to ensnare unsuspecting victims. From crafting elaborate personas to exploiting vulnerabilities, scammers utilize a range of psychological techniques to manipulate their targets. By understanding these tactics, readers can develop a heightened sense of awareness and better protect themselves against potential threats.

Identifying Fake Profiles: Red Flags to Watch Out For

Next, the focus shifts to the telltale signs of fake profiles, a common tool used by scammers to disguise their true intentions. Readers are guided through the process of identifying red flags such as minimal profile information, inconsistent details, and suspicious activity patterns. By honing their ability to discern genuine profiles from fraudulent ones, readers can mitigate the risk of falling victim to online deception.

The Art of Emotional Manipulation: How Scammers Target Your Trust

One of the most potent weapons in a scammer's arsenal is emotional manipulation. This section delves into the insidious ways in which scammers exploit their targets' emotions, preying on vulnerabilities such as loneliness, insecurity, and a desire for companionship. Through carefully crafted messages and feigned affection, scammers build a facade of trust, making it all the more challenging for victims to discern the truth. By shedding light on these manipulative tactics, readers are empowered to recognize and resist emotional manipulation, safeguarding themselves from potential harm.

Overall, Chapter 1 serves as a comprehensive guide to recognizing the signs of online deception. By delving into the tactics of social media scammers, identifying red flags in fake profiles, and understanding the nuances of emotional manipulation, readers gain invaluable insights into navigating the digital landscape with confidence and resilience. Armed with this knowledge, they can embark on their online journeys with a heightened sense of awareness, ensuring their safety and security in an ever-evolving digital world.

Chapter 2

Anatomy of a Scam: From Contact to Con

In this pivotal chapter, readers embark on a journey through the intricate web of deceit woven by online scammers, unraveling the step-by-step process from initial contact to the ultimate con. By dissecting the anatomy of a scam, readers gain a deeper understanding of the tactics employed by fraudsters, empowering them to recognize and thwart these nefarious schemes.

Initiating Contact: How Scammers Reach Out to Their Targets

The chapter opens with an exploration of the various methods scammers use to initiate contact with their targets. From leaving flattering comments on social media posts to sending unsolicited direct messages, scammers employ a range of tactics designed to pique the interest of potential victims. By understanding these initial contact strategies, readers can identify and scrutinize incoming messages, discerning genuine interactions from fraudulent ones.

Building Trust: The Rapid Rise of Affection and Flattery

Once contact is established, scammers waste no time in deploying their arsenal of charm and flattery to win over their targets. This section delves into the rapid escalation of affectionate gestures and compliments, a hallmark of many online scams. By showering their targets with attention and praise, scammers seek to cultivate a false sense of intimacy and trust, laying the groundwork for the deception to come.

Moving to Private Platforms: Why Scammers Prefer WhatsApp and Google Chat

As the relationship progresses, scammers often attempt to move the conversation to private messaging platforms such as WhatsApp or Google Chat. This shift to more secluded channels is purportedly for privacy reasons but serves the dual purpose of isolating the victim from external scrutiny. By luring their targets into these closed environments, scammers further obscure their nefarious intentions, making it increasingly difficult for victims to discern the truth.

By dissecting the anatomy of a scam, Chapter 2 equips readers with the knowledge and awareness necessary to recognize and resist the insidious tactics employed by online fraudsters. From the initial contact to the cultivation of trust and the migration to private platforms, readers gain invaluable insights into the progression of these deceptive schemes. Armed with this understanding, they are better prepared to navigate the digital landscape with vigilance and resilience, safeguarding themselves against falling prey to online scams.

Chapter 3

Tales of Deception: Stories from the Frontlines

In this chapter, readers are drawn into the compelling narratives of individuals who have fallen victim to online deception. Through firsthand accounts and real-life experiences, the chapter sheds light on the devastating impact of scams perpetrated by fraudsters operating in the digital realm. By immersing themselves in these stories, readers gain a deeper understanding of the tactics employed by scammers and the emotional toll exacted on their victims.

Military Impostors: The Uniformed Scam Artists

The chapter begins with a gripping exploration of scams perpetrated by individuals posing as members of the military. Through the lens of victims' experiences, readers gain insight into the deceptive tactics used by these impostors, from false claims of military service to the manipulation of patriotic sentiments. By delving into these stories of betrayal and deceit, readers are confronted with the stark reality of military-themed scams and the profound impact they have on those targeted.

Offshore Engineers and Boarding School Children: The Fictional Lives of Scammers

Next, readers are introduced to the elaborate personas crafted by scammers posing as offshore engineers and individuals with children in boarding schools. Drawing on personal accounts, the chapter exposes the intricacies of these fictitious identities, from fabricated professions to invented family dynamics. Through these stories, readers gain insight into the deceptive lengths to which scammers will go in pursuit of their fraudulent schemes, highlighting the need for heightened vigilance in online interactions.

The Emotional Rollercoaster: Victims' Experiences of Manipulation and Coercion

The chapter culminates with a poignant exploration of the emotional impact experienced by victims of online deception. Through firsthand testimonies, readers are immersed in the complex web of manipulation and coercion employed by scammers to exploit their targets' vulnerabilities. From feelings of betrayal and shame to the enduring psychological scars left in the wake of deception, these stories offer a sobering reminder of the human cost of online scams.

By sharing these tales of deception from the frontlines, Chapter 3 provides readers with a compelling glimpse into the lived experiences of those who have fallen victim to online scams. Through these narratives, readers gain a deeper understanding of the tactics employed by scammers and the profound emotional toll exacted on their victims. Armed with this knowledge, readers are better equipped to recognize and resist the insidious threats lurking in the digital landscape, safeguarding themselves against falling prey to online deception.

Chapter 4

Protecting Yourself: Strategies for Defense

In this pivotal chapter, readers are presented with a comprehensive toolkit of strategies and tactics aimed at fortifying their defenses against the myriad threats posed by online deception. Drawing on expert insights and real-world experiences, the chapter equips readers with the knowledge and skills necessary to safeguard their personal information, recognize fraudulent schemes, and respond effectively to potential threats.

Staying Vigilant: Tips for Recognizing and Avoiding Scams

The chapter begins with a detailed examination of the key indicators of fraudulent activity, empowering readers to sharpen their instincts and remain vigilant in their online interactions. From scrutinizing unfamiliar messages and scrutinizing suspicious profiles to verifying the authenticity of requests for personal information, readers learn to recognize the warning signs of scams and take proactive steps to protect themselves from harm.

Setting Boundaries: How to Safeguard Your Personal Information

Next, readers are guided through the process of setting and enforcing boundaries to safeguard their personal information online. By adopting a cautious approach to sharing sensitive data and implementing robust privacy settings on social media platforms, readers can minimize their exposure to potential threats and mitigate the risk of falling victim to identity theft or other forms of online fraud.

Reporting Scammers: Taking Action to Protect Yourself and Others

The chapter concludes with a call to action, urging readers to take an active role in combating online deception by reporting suspicious activity to the appropriate authorities and platform administrators. By raising awareness of fraudulent schemes and holding perpetrators accountable for their actions, readers can contribute to the collective effort to create a safer and more secure digital environment for all.

By arming readers with practical strategies for defending against online deception, Chapter 4 empowers individuals to take control of their digital security and protect themselves from potential harm. From staying vigilant and setting boundaries to reporting suspicious activity, readers gain the knowledge and confidence they need to navigate the digital landscape with resilience and peace of mind. Armed with these invaluable insights, readers can embark on their online journeys with confidence, knowing that they are equipped to defend themselves against the ever-present threats of online deception.

Chapter 5

Empowering Resilience: Reclaiming Control

In the culminating chapter of the book, readers are guided through a transformative journey of empowerment and resilience, as they learn to reclaim control over their digital lives and overcome the emotional aftermath of falling victim to online deception. Through a series of practical strategies and empowering insights, readers are encouraged to harness their inner strength and emerge from the experience with renewed confidence and resilience.

Asserting Your Rights: Saying No to Scammers' Demands

The chapter begins by empowering readers to assert their rights and boundaries in their interactions with scammers. By recognizing that they are not obligated to comply with unreasonable requests or demands for money, personal information, or other forms of assistance, readers reclaim agency over their own lives and refuse to be victimized by manipulation or coercion.

Rebuilding Trust: Recovering from the Emotional Impact of Deception

Next, readers are guided through the process of rebuilding trust in themselves and others after experiencing the emotional trauma of online deception. Through self-reflection, introspection, and perhaps seeking support from trusted friends, family members, or mental health professionals, readers begin the journey of healing and rediscovering their own resilience in the face of adversity.

Moving Forward: Strengthening Your Online Safety Practices

Finally, the chapter concludes with a call to action, encouraging readers to take proactive steps to strengthen their online safety practices and protect themselves from future threats. By implementing robust security measures, such as regularly updating passwords, enabling two-factor authentication, and staying informed about the latest scams and cybersecurity best practices, readers can reduce their vulnerability to online deception and maintain greater control over their digital lives.

By embracing the principles of empowerment and resilience outlined in Chapter 5, readers emerge from the experience of online deception stronger, wiser, and more resilient than ever before. Through self-assertion, emotional healing, and proactive safety measures, readers reclaim control over their digital destinies and forge a path forward with confidence and resilience. Armed with these invaluable insights and tools, readers are empowered to navigate the digital landscape with courage and resilience, knowing that they have the knowledge and strength to overcome any challenge that comes their way.

Discussion Questions

1. How do you perceive the evolution of online scams and deception tactics over time, and what implications does this have for individuals' digital safety?

2. Reflecting on the chapter about recognizing the signs of online deception, have you ever encountered suspicious behavior online, and how did you respond?

3. In Chapter 2, the anatomy of a scam is dissected from initial contact to the final con. What aspects of this process surprised you the most, and how do you think scammers exploit human psychology to achieve their goals?

4. Chapter 3 delves into real-life stories of individuals who have fallen victim to online deception. How do these narratives shape your understanding of the emotional toll of scams, and what lessons can be learned from their experiences?

5. As discussed in Chapter 4, what proactive measures do you take to protect yourself from online deception, and how do you balance engagement with caution in your online interactions?

6. In Chapter 5, the concept of empowering resilience is explored. How do you think individuals can cultivate resilience in the face of online deception, and what role does community support play in this process?

7. Drawing on the discussion about Amazon backend keywords, how important do you think it is for authors to optimize their book listings to enhance discoverability, and what strategies would you recommend for effective keyword selection?

8. Considering the broader societal impact of online deception, how can education and awareness initiatives help empower individuals to recognize and resist scams, and what role do policymakers and tech companies play in addressing this issue?

Reflection Essay

In today's interconnected world, where social media platforms serve as gateways to global communication and connection, the prevalence of online deception poses a significant challenge. As I reflect on the insights gained from exploring the anatomy of online scams, the emotional toll on victims, and strategies for defense, I am struck by the complex interplay between trust, vulnerability, and resilience in the digital realm.

The journey begins with an exploration of the tactics used by scammers to initiate contact and cultivate trust. From flattering comments to private messaging, the methods employed are as varied as they are insidious. Through emotional manipulation and the creation of false personas, scammers exploit the very human desire for connection, leaving victims vulnerable to exploitation.

As we delve deeper into the stories of those who have fallen victim to online deception, the human cost becomes painfully clear. The emotional rollercoaster of manipulation and coercion leaves lasting scars, challenging victims to rebuild trust in themselves and others. Yet, amidst the darkness, there are glimmers of resilience—stories of individuals who refuse to be defined by their experiences, who reclaim agency over their digital lives and empower others to do the same.

In the face of such pervasive threats, Chapter 4 emerges as a beacon of hope, offering practical strategies for defense. From staying vigilant and setting boundaries to reporting suspicious activity, readers are empowered to take control of their digital security and protect themselves from harm. Through education and awareness, we arm ourselves with the knowledge and skills necessary to navigate the digital landscape with confidence and resilience.

As I consider the broader implications of online deception, I am reminded of the importance of collective action. By sharing our stories, raising awareness, and advocating for change, we can create a safer and more secure digital environment for all. Whether through community support networks or policy initiatives, we have the power to confront online deception head-on and protect those most vulnerable to its effects.

In conclusion, navigating the digital landscape requires a delicate balance of trust, vigilance, and resilience. By recognizing the signs of online deception, supporting those affected, and empowering individuals to defend themselves, we can foster a culture of digital safety and accountability. Together, we can turn the tide against online deception and build a more trustworthy and inclusive online world for future generations.

www.ingramcontent.com/pod-product-compliance
Lightning Source LLC
Chambersburg PA
CBHW070956220526
45471CB00007B/3060